Djokovic Novak

Biography of a successful tennis player

Author: Alia Bouta

ALIAREDA © 2023

All worldwide rights of reproduction, adaptation and translation, in whole or in part, are reserved. The author is the sole owner of the rights and responsible for the content of this book.

book plan

- BOOK PLAN -------- 2
- INTRODUCTION -------- 3
1. WHO IS NOVAK DJOKOVIS? -------- 8
2. THE EARLY YEARS -------- 14
3. RISING THROUGH THE JUNIOR RANKS -------- 18
4. TRANSITION TO THE PROFESSIONAL CIRCUIT -------- 23
5. EARLY SUCCESSES AND BREAKTHROUGH MOMENTS -------- 29
6. EVOLUTION AND CONTINUED DOMINANCE -------- 35
7. RISING THROUGH THE RANKS -------- 40
8. THE BIG THREE ERA: DJOKOVIC'S RIVALRY WITH FEDERER AND NADAL -------- 46
9. GRAND SLAM GLORY: NOVAK DJOKOVIC'S QUEST FOR TENNIS IMMORTALITY -------- 52
10. THE INTENSE RIVALRIES OF NOVAK DJOKOVIC -------- 58
11. UNVEILING THE GLORIOUS TROPHIES OF NOVAK DJOKOVIC -------- 63
12. THE STATISTICAL DOMINANCE OF NOVAK DJOKOVIC -------- 68
13. THE RISE OF NOVAK DJOKOVIC'S BUSINESS EMPIRE -------- 73
14. MENTAL FORTITUDE: THE UNBREAKABLE SPIRIT OF NOVAK DJOKOVIC -------- 79
15. A COMPARISON BETWEEN NOVAK DJOKOVIC AND OTHER TENNIS PLAYERS -------- 84
16. THE KEY FACTORS BEHIND NOVAK DJOKOVIC'S SUCCESS AND FAILURE -------- 90
17. THE ART OF STYLE PLAY: DECODING NOVAK DJOKOVIC'S SIGNATURE TENNIS FASHION -------- 97
18. THE UNSTOPPABLE LEGACY OF NOVAK DJOKOVIC -------- 102
19. THE PRIVATE LIFE OF NOVAK DJOKOVIC -------- 108
20. THE UNFATHOMABLE FORTUNE OF NOVAK DJOKOVIC 113
21. THE UNPARALLELED RECORDS OF NOVAK DJOKOVIC -------- 118
22. THE ENIGMATIC PERSONA OF NOVAK DJOKOVIC -------- 123
23. THE JOURNEY TO BECOMING LIKE NOVAK DJOKOVIC 128
24. THE MULTI-FACETED WORLD OF NOVAK DJOKOVIC'S HOBBIES -------- 134
- CONCLUSION -------- 139

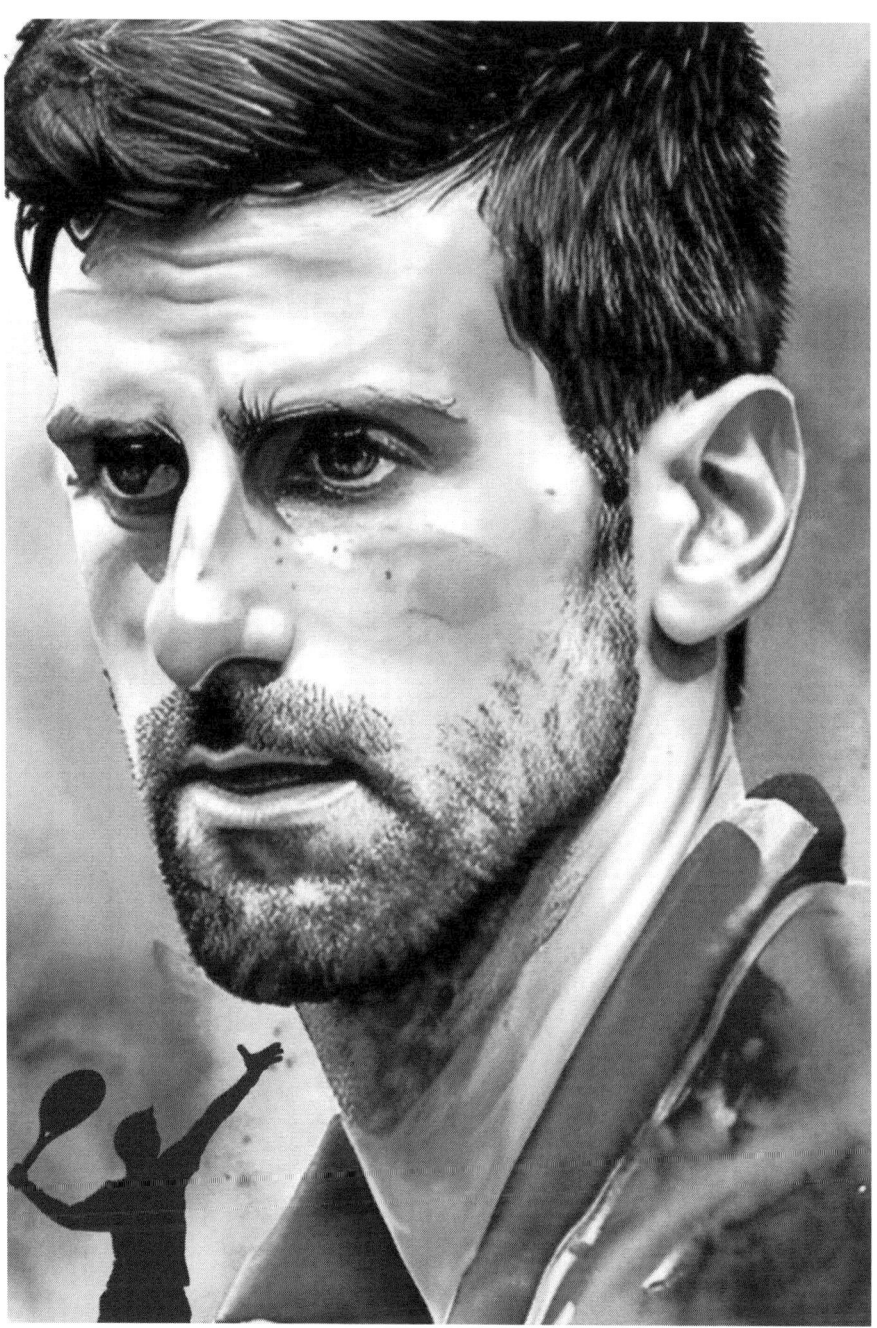

Introduction

Novak Djokovic is one of the few names in tennis history that make you think of unwavering determination, unwavering passion, and an unstoppable spirit. Djokovic is on a remarkable path to becoming one of the best athletes of the 21st century. He is a great tennis player and has an unmatched ability to overcome problems.

In this book, we learn a lot about the life of this tennis prodigy who was born in Serbia. This carefully written biography takes us on a fascinating journey that tells the story of how Djokovic went from living in a war-torn area to becoming a shining star in the tennis world.

From his humble beginnings as a young boy bouncing tennis balls off the walls of an improvised court in Belgrade to his epic battles against the tennis world's biggest names,

Djokovic's story is one of resilience, perseverance, and unwavering determination. We see how his family never gave up on him, how much they sacrificed, and how Djokovic never stopped believing that he could reach his childhood dreams.

But this biography is about much more than just wins and trophies. It looks at how Djokovic's mind works as he moves through the complicated world of professional tennis. We talk about the many hours of sweat and sacrifice he put into getting better at what he did, the mental battles he fought on the tennis court, and the personal struggles that tested his strength on and off the court.

"The Unbreakable Spirit" tells about parts of Djokovic's life that aren't as well known, like his passion for helping others, his search for self-discovery, and his unwavering commitment to promoting unity and peace in a divided world.

We learn about the man behind the tennis legend, get a look into the heart of a winner, and see how much of an impact he has had on and off the court.

This book is full of interesting stories, insightful thoughts, and exclusive interviews with people who know Djokovic well. It promises to be an immersive reading experience that will keep tennis fans interested and inspire dreamers. Through the pages of "The Unbreakable Spirit," readers will learn how this extraordinary athlete changed tennis, redefined power, and etched his name into the halls of sporting greatness.

Prepare to be amazed, inspired, and enthralled as we take a fascinating journey through the life and relentless spirit of Novak Djokovic, an athlete who broke records, broke rules, and left an indelible mark on the world of tennis and beyond.

1. Who is Novak Djokovis?

Novak Djokovic was born in Belgrade, Serbia, on May 22, 1987. He is a professional tennis player who is widely thought to be one of the best ever. Djokovic has overcome many obstacles to become one of the best tennis players in the world. He has done this by being very determined, having great skills, and working hard all the time.

Djokovic started playing tennis at a very young age. He started training at age 4. His parents, Srdjan and Dijana, saw how talented he was and encouraged him to pursue a career in sports. Djokovic worked with a number of coaches, including the famous Serbian tennis player Jelena Gencic, who saw his huge potential and helped him train.

As a young player, Djokovic made a name for himself quickly in Serbia and around the world. Tennis fans were impressed by his natural talent, lightning-fast footwork, and powerful groundstrokes. Djokovic won several junior titles, which showed that he was a tough opponent.

Djokovic turned pro in 2003, when he was only 16 years old. This was the start of an amazing journey. At first, it wasn't easy for him to get to the top of tennis, but his incredible work ethic and determination helped him get there.

In 2008, when he won his first Grand Slam title at the Australian Open, Djokovic became well-known. Djokovic showed how talented and tough he is by beating the legendary Roger Federer in the semifinals and the Frenchman Jo-Wilfried Tsonga in the final. This victory was the start of a long and successful career, as well as a rivalry with Roger Federer and Rafael Nadal that would define an era.

Over the years, Djokovic has been the best player on the court. He has won a number of Grand Slam titles, including nine at the Australian Open, five at Wimbledon, three at the US Open, and two at the French Open. The fact that he has won every major tournament shows how flexible, adaptable, and mentally strong he is.

Besides winning Grand Slams, Djokovic has reached many other important points in his career. He was the world's best player for a record-setting 325 weeks, beating Federer and Nadal's previous record. Djokovic also became the first player to win all nine ATP Masters 1000 tournaments. This made him one of the best tennis players of all time.

Djokovic is known for his intensity on the court. He plays with amazing speed, perfect footwork, and a strong two-handed backhand. Because it was so easy for him to turn defense into offense, people called him "Djoker" because of how good he was at returning serves and playing defense. Djokovic has been able to win many long matches and make amazing comebacks because he has a strong mind and can perform well under pressure.

Off the court, Djokovic is known for his charitable work and his desire to help his community. In 2007, he started the Novak Djokovic Foundation, which helps young children in Serbia get an education and gives them opportunities. Djokovic also uses his fame to bring attention to environmental issues and encourage people to live healthier lives.Novak Djokovic has had a huge effect on the world of tennis. Fans and other players alike respect and admire him for how hard he works, how professional he is, and how much he loves the sport. As long as he keeps playing at the highest level, Djokovic will always be remembered as one of the best tennis players of all time.

2. The Early Years

Novak Djokovic's path to becoming a tennis prodigy started when he was young. That's when he started to love and care about the sport. As a child growing up in Belgrade, Serbia, Djokovic was exposed to tennis by his family and the people around him.

Srdjan and Dijana, Djokovic's parents, did a lot to help him develop his talent and follow his dreams. They saw that he was naturally good at tennis and encouraged him to keep doing it from a very young age. Srdjan, Djokovic's father, used to ski professionally, and Dijana, Djokovic's mother, worked at a sports academy. Because they had been athletes before, they knew how much dedication and hard work it takes to do well in any sport.

Even when he was young, Djokovic showed that he was

very focused, determined, and had a natural talent for the game. He would practice for hours by hitting a tennis ball against the walls of a nearby tennis court. This helped him get better at tennis before he even went to a real tennis court. Djokovic's family saw how talented he was and put him in the local tennis club right away. There, he got his first formal training.

At the tennis club, Djokovic's skill was clear right away. His coaches were amazed by how quickly he could learn new techniques and use them. Djokovic had great hand-eye coordination and footwork, which let him move around the court quickly and easily. He is known as a tennis prodigy because of his quick reflexes and agility, which set him apart from his peers.

As Djokovic's love for tennis grew, he would often copy the ways they played and the shots they used. He would look at the strokes of great tennis players like Pete Sampras and Andre Agassi and try to copy them on the court. The young prodigy was known for his determination to learn new things and add them to his game.

Djokovic's relationship with his coach, Jelena Gencic, was one of the most important things that helped him become a tennis prodigy. Gencic took Djokovic under her wing when she first saw how talented he was. She was very important in helping Djokovic improve his technical skills and mental strength. Gencic's role as a mentor gave Djokovic the advice and help he needed to make it in the tough world of professional tennis.

Even though he was young, Djokovic was very competitive and hungry for success. He played in both local and national junior tournaments, where his skill level and calmness on the court amazed his opponents. Djokovic's quick rise through the junior ranks showed off how talented he was and set him up for future success.

Djokovic's early years as a tennis player helped him become the prodigy he would become. His family's constant support, his desire to keep getting better, and the advice of his coaches helped him build a strong foundation for his future success. These experiences helped Djokovic develop his skills and gave him the drive to become one of the best tennis players of all time.

3. Rising Through the Junior Ranks

Novak Djokovic's early success as a tennis prodigy was proven as he quickly rose through the junior ranks, catching the attention of tennis fans and professionals all over the world. During these formative years, Djokovic's natural talent and hard work started to pay off, making him one of the sport's most promising young players.

Djokovic's game kept getting better and better as he worked hard and took advice from his coaches. He worked hard to improve his technique, his footwork, and his mental toughness. Djokovic stands out from his peers because he can play on different types of courts and is good at playing strategically.

Djokovic broke through on the junior circuit after a series

of strong showings in big tournaments. He won several titles, which showed off his amazing skills and brought him a lot of attention. These wins not only gave him more confidence, but also showed that all the hard work and sacrifices he had made over the years to follow his dreams were worth it.

As Djokovic's fame grew, he became more successful outside of his home country, Serbia. He started playing in international tournaments for juniors, where he faced talented players from all over the world. Not only did these situations test his skills, but they also gave him a chance to learn about different ways of playing and cultures.

During these junior tournaments, Djokovic showed how competitive he is and how focused he is all the time. He became known for how hard he worked and how he never gave up, even when things got hard. Djokovic started to stand out because of how strong he was mentally. He was able to deal with problems and beat very skilled opponents.

Djokovic was a great player technically, but he was also very aware of the court and had great tactical skills. He had an uncanny ability to figure out how his opponents played and change his strategy on the spot. Djokovic's smart shot choices and ability to put together points with precision showed how smart he was at tennis and how much talent he had.

Djokovic's rise through the junior ranks helped him get ready for the professional tennis circuit. His success in junior tournaments not only gave him more confidence, but also got him into professional tournaments as a "wild card." This gave him a chance to play against more experienced pros, which he found very helpful.

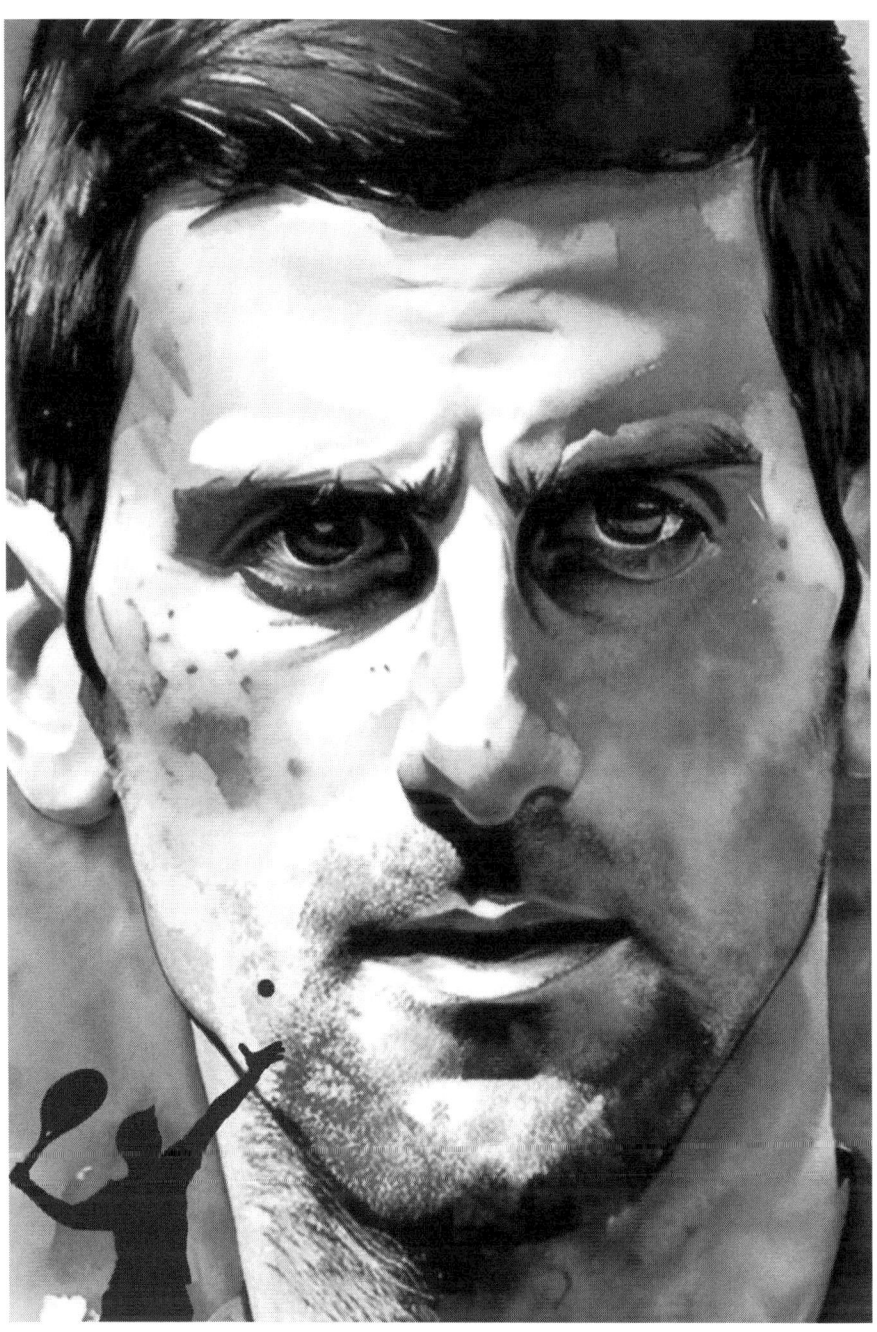

Djokovic never lost sight of his goals during this time. His commitment, discipline, and desire to get better never changed. He kept working hard on his game, always improving his skills and getting in better physical and mental shape.

Djokovic's rising success on the junior circuit showed that he had a lot of talent, worked hard all the time, and never gave up. These early years set the stage for his later successes and helped him rise to become one of the best tennis players of all time.

4. Transition to the Professional Circuit

Novak Djokovic went from being a tennis prodigy to a powerful player on the professional circuit because he worked hard to be the best, kept his mind strong, and never stopped believing in himself. After becoming the best junior player in the world, Djokovic set his sights on becoming one of the best players in the world.

Djokovic's move from amateur tennis to professional tennis was not without its problems. As a young player, he had to show what he could do against seasoned pros who had been playing for years. Djokovic made an immediate impression on the court because of how calm and in control he was and how good he was.

In 2007, when he made it to the final of the US Open, which was his first Grand Slam final, it was one of Djokovic's first big breaks. Even though he lost in the final to Roger Federer, who was the best player in the world at the time, Djokovic showed that he was ready for the big time. Tennis fans and experts were amazed by his level of skill and maturity, which was way above his age.

After he did well at the US Open, Djokovic kept making a name for himself on the professional circuit. He kept up a consistent level of play and won several ATP Tour events, which helped him slowly move up the rankings. Djokovic made a lot of progress because he worked hard and was able to quickly change his game to fit different situations.

2008 was a turning point in Djokovic's career as a tennis player. At the Australian Open, he won his first Grand Slam title by beating the French player Jo-Wilfried Tsonga in a tough final. With this win, Djokovic moved up to the top of men's tennis and solidified his reputation as a strong contender.

With his first Grand Slam win, Djokovic's confidence went through the roof, and he set his sights on even more success. He started to challenge tennis legends Roger Federer and Rafael Nadal, who had been the best men's players for a long time.

2011 turned out to be a turning point for Djokovic. He had an amazing season, winning three of the four Grand Slam titles and going 70-6 for the year. Djokovic's strong mind and constant drive for perfection were on full display as he consistently did better than his opponents and overcame key points of pressure.

During this amazing streak, Djokovic also became the

world's best player for the first time in his career. He was the first player since 1993 to beat both Federer and Nadal. This showed that he was the best player in the world when two of the best ever were at their best.

Djokovic was successful not only because he was good at tennis physically, but also because he was strong mentally. He showed that he was a strong opponent in high-pressure situations by always coming out on top in long, tough matches that tested his mental and physical strength.

As Djokovic continued to show that he was the best professional tennis player, he showed a lot of consistency by successfully defending his Grand Slam titles and staying at the top of the tennis world for a longer time. He was one of the sport's true champions because he worked hard to be the best and could step up his game when it mattered.

The fact that Djokovic went from being a tennis prodigy to a professional star shows how talented, sure of himself, and hardworking he is. His ability to play so well against the best players in the world cemented his place as one of tennis' top players and set the stage for an amazing career full of records and accomplishments.

5. Early Successes and Breakthrough Moments

Novak Djokovic's professional career has been marked by a number of early wins and breakthroughs that have shown off his huge talent and propelled him to the top of tennis. Djokovic's achievements during this time solidified his place among the best tennis players and set the stage for his future dominance. These achievements built on his impressive transition from a tennis prodigy to a professional player.

In 2008, when Djokovic won his first Grand Slam tournament, the Australian Open, his confidence and faith in his skills went through the roof. He kept showing off his great skills and mental toughness on the court, always beating his opponents and leaving the crowd in awe.

In 2010, Djokovic won his second Grand Slam title at the Australian Open. This was one of the best things to happen during this time. In an exciting final, he beat Andy Murray, who was the defending champion and the best player in the world at the time. As he fought his way to a thrilling victory, Djokovic showed how determined and determined to win he is.

Djokovic's win at the 2010 Australian Open was a big step in his career. It showed that he could keep doing well on the biggest stages of tennis. With this win, he proved that he was a serious contender in Grand Slam tournaments and solidified his place as one of the best tennis players in the world.

In 2011, at the Wimbledon Championships, Djokovic had another big break-through moment. Djokovic beat his opponents on the grass courts with his aggressive and accurate game. This got him to the final. In the championship match against Rafael Nadal, he showed great skill, toughness, and mental strength, and in the end, he won in a thrilling four-set match. This win was not only Djokovic's first at Wimbledon, but it also cemented his reputation as a strong player on all surfaces.

In the same amazing year, Djokovic did something that had never been done before: he won three of the four Grand Slam titles. The best part of this amazing achievement was when he beat Rafael Nadal in the final of the US Open. This showed how well he could adapt to hard courts. Djokovic's performance of unwavering determination and tenacity showed how strong he is and cemented his place as one of the best athletes of all time.

Djokovic's early successes and breakthroughs were made possible by his great skills and unwavering confidence in himself. The established order of men's tennis was shaken up by his ability to win on different playing surfaces and his mental and tactical skills. Djokovic's play took him to new heights and earned him a lot of respect and admiration from tennis players and fans all over the world.

These accomplishments not only showed how talented Djokovic was, but they also started a fierce rivalry with other tennis greats like Roger Federer and Rafael Nadal, which led to a golden age for men's tennis. Djokovic's ability to consistently challenge and beat these strong opponents raised the level of competition in the sport and made their matches more interesting.

In a nutshell, Djokovic's early successes and breakthroughs were important turning points in his career. These accomplishments not only cemented his place as one of the best in his sport, but also made him a serious contender in Grand Slam tournaments. Djokovic's great talent, unwavering belief, and never-ending pursuit of excellence set the stage for an amazing career full of many accomplishments and records.

6. Evolution and Continued Dominance

As Djokovic's career went on, he kept getting better as a player by always working on his skills and changing how he played based on the conditions. This change, along with his constant drive and determination, has helped him keep being the best tennis player in the world.

His serve is one part of his game that has changed in a noticeable way over the years. He has worked hard to make his serve stronger and more accurate. This has helped him control the game and win more free points. Djokovic's improved serving has not only helped him do better overall, but it has also made his opponents work harder.

Djokovic's continued success has also been helped by the fact that he has a strong mind. He is very good at staying calm and collected under pressure, and he often plays his best tennis when the stakes are high. Djokovic's mental strength has helped him come back from what seemed like impossible situations and win matches, leaving his opponents stunned and spectators in awe.

Djokovic has done well as an individual player, but he has also become a very strong team player. He has been a key member of the Serbian national team, which won the Davis Cup in 2010 and 2021 with his help. Djokovic's leadership and talent have been key to Serbia's success, and he is often credited with pushing his teammates to do their best.

Djokovic's dominance on all playing surfaces is another thing that stands out about his career. Some players are better on one surface than another, but Djokovic has always played at the highest level on hard, grass, and clay courts. This makes him stand out from a lot of his competitors and shows how adaptable and flexible he is as a player.

Djokovic's constant drive to be the best has also made him more disciplined and physically fit. He has spent a lot of time getting fit and in shape, which lets him play long, tough matches and beat his opponents. Djokovic's physical strength and technical skill have made him a tough opponent and a hard player to beat.

Djokovic's continued success is also due to the fact that he is committed to living a healthy life and sticking to a strict diet. He is known for his gluten-free, mostly plant-based diet, which he says has helped him feel healthier and have more energy. Djokovic's care for his physical and mental health shows how dedicated he is to staying at his best on and off the court.

As Djokovic's career has grown, he has broken many records and reached many milestones. He has spent more weeks at the top of the ATP rankings than anyone else. Roger Federer and Rafael Nadal held the record before him. Djokovic also became the first player in the Open Era to win all four Grand Slam titles twice. This added to the fact that he is one of the best tennis players of all time.

In the end, Djokovic's continued dominance in the tennis world is a result of how he has grown as a player and how determined and strong-minded he is. His improved serve, mental toughness, physical fitness, and ability to play on any surface have helped him consistently beat his competitors and reach heights in the sport that have never been reached before. Djokovic will be a force to be reckoned with for many years to come because he never stops trying to be the best.

7. Rising Through the Ranks

Novak Djokovic's rise to the top of the tennis world was nothing short of amazing. From his early days as a talented junior player to his big break on the international stage, Djokovic's rise to the top showed how skilled, determined, and dedicated he was to tennis.

As a young tennis player in Serbia, Djokovic's natural talent made coaches and other players take notice of him right away. Djokovic started training hard at a young age, with the help of his parents. His hard work and dedication paid off quickly, and he soon started doing very well in national and regional tournaments.

In 2001, when he was only 14, Djokovic won the Australian Open Boys' Singles title. This was his big break on the international junior tennis circuit. This win brought him to the attention of tennis fans and experts all over the world, who saw his great potential.

In the years that followed, Djokovic continued to make a name for himself on the junior tennis circuit. He won a few more titles and got noticed for his technical skills, quick footwork, and powerful groundstrokes. As his reputation grew, tennis academies and professional coaches became interested in him and wanted to help him improve.

For Djokovic, the turning point came when he started to work with Jelena Gencic, a Serbian coach. Under Gencic's guidance, he quickly got better at his game, especially in terms of mental toughness and thinking strategically. Not only did she help him improve his skills, but she also gave him the strength he needed to deal with the challenges of professional tennis.

Djokovic turned pro when he was 16 and started his journey on the ATP Tour. At first, it was hard for him to move up to the professional level because he had to play against more experienced and stronger players. But Djokovic's strong self-confidence and drive helped him move forward.

In 2006, he reached the quarterfinals of the French Open, beating several top-ranked players along the way. This was his first big break as a professional. This performance made him a rising star and was the start of his steady climb up the rankings.

Over the next few years, Djokovic kept getting better and better at his game. He never stopped working hard, and that, along with his powerful groundstrokes and perfect court coverage, helped him reach the top of his sport over time. He always showed that he could compete at the highest level, putting Roger Federer and Rafael Nadal's dominance in tennis to the test.

In 2008, Djokovic won his first Grand Slam title at the Australian Open by beating Jo-Wilfried Tsonga in the final. This was a big moment for him. This win not only showed that he had arrived as a major player in men's tennis, but it also marked the start of an era in which Djokovic, Federer, and Nadal would fight fiercely for the top spots in the sport.

Djokovic's confidence and desire to win kept growing as the years went by, and so did his ranking. He always pushed himself to reach new heights. He was always trying to improve his game and do better. His breakthroughs and victories showed how determined and strong-willed he was, and they inspired a new generation of tennis players.

In the years that followed, Djokovic won a lot of Grand Slams and became the best male tennis player in the world. But it was his early years, when he worked his way up and overcame problems, that set the stage for him to become a great leader. Djokovic went from being a talented young player in Serbia to a tennis superstar around the world. This shows how talented, dedicated, and driven he is.

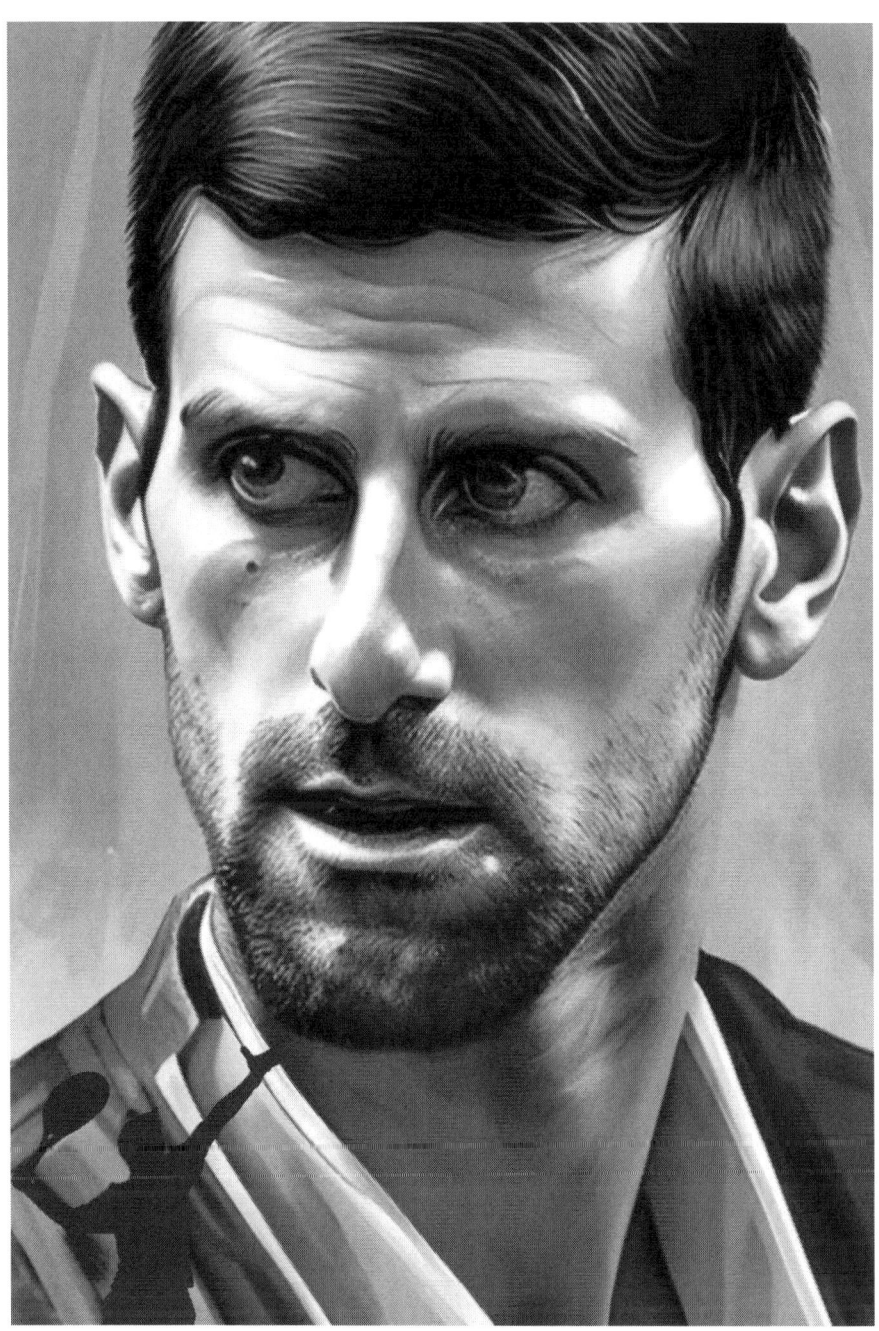

8. The Big Three Era: Djokovic's Rivalry with Federer and Nadal

Novak Djokovic came on the tennis scene during the Big Three era, which was dominated by three very good players. Together with Roger Federer and Rafael Nadal, Djokovic was part of a trio that changed the sport. Their exciting matches captured the world's attention and rewrote the record books. This chapter looks at Djokovic's fierce competition with Federer and Nadal, how their careers affected each other, and what they all brought to the game as a whole.

Djokovic, Federer, and Nadal all had different ways of playing the game, and each had their own strengths and ways of doing things. Federer was the picture of elegance and grace with his smooth strokes and perfect shots. Nadal, on the other hand, became known for his relentless power and fierce determination in his pursuit of success. On the other hand, Djokovic was known for his amazing flexibility, unbeatable defense, and ability to get back shots that seemed impossible. Their different ways of doing things made every time they met unpredictable and very entertaining.

As Djokovic moved up the ranks, he became a constant pain in Federer and Nadal's sides by challenging their supremacy on the court. Their matches were at their most intense during the Grand Slams, where they fought epic battles that changed what it meant to compete. During the Big Three era, these matches became some of the most exciting in tennis history. For example, Djokovic beat Federer in the US Open semifinals in 2010, and he beat Nadal in five sets in the Australian Open final in 2012.

The rivalry between the three went beyond just numbers

and statistics. Their matches were full of exciting drama, never-ending hard work, and a strong will to win. From Wimbledon classics that pushed the limits of endurance, like Djokovic's win over Federer in the 2019 final, to spine-tingling battles at Roland Garros, where Djokovic and Nadal met in multiple finals, their matches have etched themselves into the history of great sports.

Even though Djokovic, Federer, and Nadal were fierce rivals on the court, they had a lot of respect and admiration for each other off the court. They kept raising the bar for what was possible in the sport by pushing each other to do better. Their combined dominance took men's tennis to levels that had never been seen before and started an era of amazing tennis that will be remembered for years to come.

As the Big Three era went on, Djokovic, Federer, and

Nadal won an incredible number of Grand Slam titles and wrote their names into the history of tennis. Djokovic's constant drive for excellence helped him stay at the top of the ATP rankings for a long time, which put him in competition with Federer and Nadal's records. They not only broke records, but they also showed aspiring tennis players all over the world that they could be great if they were determined, worked hard, and never gave up.

Tennis fans will always remember the time when Novak Djokovic, Roger Federer, and Rafael Nadal were known as the "Big Three." The fierce battles they fought on the court went beyond their personal rivalries. They captivated people all over the world and left an indelible mark on the history of the sport. Djokovic's role in this era was important because he worked hard to prove that he was on the same level as these legendary tennis players. Men's tennis will never be the same because of what these three players did for the sport as a whole, not just what they did for themselves.

9. Grand Slam Glory: Novak Djokovic's Quest for Tennis Immortality

Novak Djokovic's journey to Grand Slam glory shows how good he is, how hard he works, and how determined he is. In this chapter, we look at the most memorable parts of Djokovic's career, as he wins the most prestigious tennis tournaments in the world and joins the sport's greatest legends in the record books.

A. The Turning Point: Winning the 2008 Australian Open

- Djokovic wins his first major title in Melbourne. This is his first Grand Slam win.
- Beating Roger Federer in the semifinals and Jo-Wilfried Tsonga in the final.

- Making a name for himself among the "Big Three" players, Federer, Rafael Nadal, and Djokovic.

B. Historic 2011 Season: A Year of Success Never Seen Before

- Djokovic's incredible run, in which he won three Grand Slam titles in a single year, which broke a record.
- Beating Rafael Nadal in the finals of the US Open, Wimbledon, and the Australian Open.
- Going on an amazing 41-match winning streak, which took his game to a whole new level.

C. The Nerves of Steel: The Epic 2012 Australian Open Final

- Djokovic and Rafael Nadal's epic battle in the longest major final ever played.
- In an exciting match that lasted almost six hours, Djokovic came out on top.

- Showing a level of mental toughness, resilience, and faith in his abilities that was unmatched.

D. "The Djokovic Slam": Winning all four Grand Slams in a career

- Djokovic's constant effort to win at Roland Garros, which is the only major trophy he doesn't have yet.
- Making it to the final of the 2016 French Open and beating Andy Murray.
- Solidifying his place as one of the best players of all time by becoming only the eighth person to win a Career Grand Slam.

E. Epic 2019 Wimbledon Final: "Battle of the Titans"

- A rematch with Federer in a Wimbledon final for the ages.
- Djokovic's unwavering determination and brilliant strategy in a historic five-set thriller.

- Djokovic's victory in the longest Wimbledon final ever played, in which he saved two match points.

F. F. Chasing History: The Search for the Grand Slam Record

- Djokovic is trying to beat Federer and Nadal's record of 20 Grand Slam titles.
- Beating Federer's record for most weeks as world number one.
- Setting his sights on becoming the best of all time, driven by an unquenchable desire to win.

Novak Djokovic has become a tennis legend because he has won so many grand slams. His constant drive to be the best, incredible mental strength, and incredible athleticism have helped him win on the biggest stages of his sport. As Djokovic keeps trying to make history, he is a force to be reckoned with because he is so driven and has so much talent. With each Grand Slam win, Djokovic's name gets deeper into tennis history, cementing his place as one of the sport's all-time greats.

10. The Intense Rivalries of Novak Djokovic

Novak Djokovic has had a great tennis career full of fierce rivalries that have pushed him to new heights and given the sport some exciting moments. These rivalries have not only shown how competitive Djokovic is, but they have also given tennis fans some of the most exciting and memorable matches in the sport's history. In this chapter, we'll look at some of Djokovic's most intense rivalries that have changed the tennis world for good.

Stan Wawrinka, a Swiss tennis player, has been one of Djokovic's most interesting opponents. Over the years, these two tennis greats have faced off in epic matches that have kept fans on the edge of their seats.

Djokovic had to deal with Wawrinka's powerful

groundstrokes and his ability to hit winners from anywhere on the court. Their matches were full of hard-hitting rallies and hard-hitting shots, and both players pushed each other to their physical and mental limits.

The best match between Djokovic and Wawrinka took place in the fourth round of the 2013 Australian Open. This match is often called one of the best in Grand Slam history. The match lasted more than five hours and was full of amazing shots and unwavering determination from both players. In the end, Djokovic won a thrilling five-set battle.

Novak Djokovic's rivalry with rising star Alexander Zverev is a great example of the fierce competition between a seasoned champion and a young player with a lot of potential. Zverev was a tough opponent for Djokovic because of his strong serve and aggressive style of play.

Because they are rivals, they have played each other in many high-stakes matches, like the 2020 ATP Cup final, where Zverev was a key part of Team Germany's win over Team Serbia. These matches have shown how different players' styles are and how the sport has changed as Djokovic faces players from the next generation.

Djokovic's rivalry with Austrian tennis star Dominic Thiem is a more recent one that has been getting a lot of attention. Thiem's aggressive baseline play and ability to hit powerful groundstrokes made his matches with Djokovic very tough and full of exciting rallies.

The Australian Open finals in 2020 and 2021 were the pinnacle of their rivalry. In 2020, Djokovic won by beating Thiem in a five-set match that showed how athletic and good at making shots both players were. Thiem got his own back the next year, though, when he beat Djokovic in another tough five-set final.

The battles between Djokovic and Thiem have sparked the race for Grand Slam titles, with both players eager to show how good they are on tennis's biggest stages.

In the end, Novak Djokovic's tennis career has been shaped by fierce rivalries that have kept him going. From his fights with Wawrinka and Zverev, which showed the clash of generations, to his tense matches with Thiem, who represents Grand Slam glory, Djokovic has always faced strong opponents who have pushed him to improve his game. These rivalries have given tennis fans exciting matches that will be remembered for a long time. These rivalries, with their fierce competition and memorable moments, have had a big impact on Djokovic's unbreakable spirit and helped him become one of the best tennis players of all time.

11. Unveiling the Glorious Trophies of Novak Djokovic

Novak Djokovic is known for being the best tennis player ever, and he has won a huge number of trophies over the course of his long career. These reminders of how hard he worked and how much he wanted to be the best showed that he was the best player on the court. As we look through Djokovic's long list of awards, we are welcomed into a world where dreams came true and where winning became a well-known friend.

The Grand Slam Crown, which sparkled on a grand stand, proved that Djokovic was the undisputed king of tennis. This regal trophy was made of solid gold and studded with a stunning array of precious gems. It showed how much work and dedication it took to win a Grand Slam. It had four intricate emblems that stood for the Australian

Open, the French Open, Wimbledon, and the US Open. It was a physical reminder of how far Djokovic had come in tennis, making him a true king of the sport.

The Golden Racquet of Immortality was kept in a shiny glass case that made everyone who saw it look at it. Made of the best materials and shining gold, this work of art went beyond being useful and became a symbol of Djokovic's unmatched skill. This racquet was like Excalibur because it was used by the Serbian champion to beat tough opponents and make his name a part of tennis history. Its handle, which was covered in intricate engravings, told stories of Djokovic's many victories, which showed why it was one of his most prized trophies.

Djokovic was proud of his Serbian roots, so he held a special trophy that honored not only his own wins but also the spirit of his beloved country.

This powerful trophy was called the Serb Shield of Perseverance. It had the Serbian coat of arms and a list of Djokovic's accomplishments etched into its silver surface. Every time Djokovic had a moment of doubt, this shield reminded him of how determined he was. Each victory showed how strong his spirit was and how determined his people were.

The Eternal Timepiece was put in a place of honor and rested on a bed of clean velvet. This trophy was a work of art. It was made with the precision of a Swiss watchmaker, and every detail showed Djokovic's journey through time. The sparkling diamonds on the central dial showed how many hours of hard work he had put into his craft. The hands moved with grace and precision, which reminded everyone who saw it how precious every moment of Djokovic's career is. The Eternal Timepiece was a celebration of time, a tribute to the countless hours Djokovic had spent perfecting his craft, and a reminder to enjoy every victory he had won.

These beautiful trophies, each with its own story and meaning, gave a glimpse into Novak Djokovic's unstoppable spirit. These trophies showed Djokovic's successful journey, which was built on a love for the sport, fueled by an insatiable desire to win, and guided by an unwavering desire to be the best. With each trophy, Djokovic's legacy grew, and people all over the world were amazed by what he did on the tennis court.

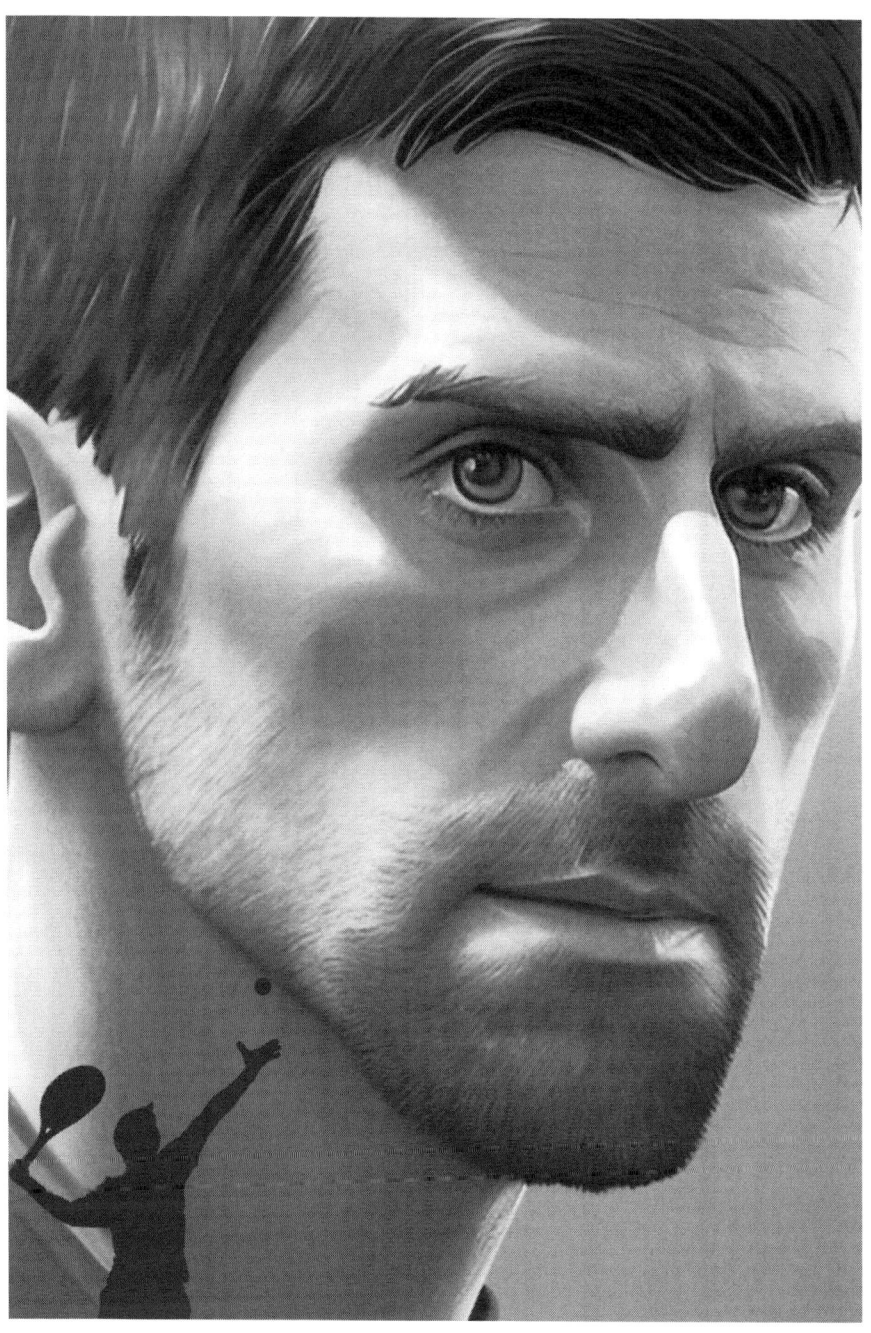

12. The Statistical Dominance of Novak Djokovic

Novak Djokovic, a tennis star from Serbia, has firmly established himself as one of the best players in the history of the sport. Over the years, Djokovic has always shown on the court his amazing skills, mental toughness, and unmatched consistency. In this chapter, we look at Novak Djokovic's statistical skills by looking at his career accomplishments, records, and statistical milestones that show how great he is.

Novak Djokovic's incredible success in winning all four Grand Slam titles shows how hard he works to be the best. As of 2021, Djokovic has won a whopping 20 Grand Slam singles titles, putting him on par with Roger Federer and Rafael Nadal, two of the best tennis players of all time. There are nine Australian Open titles, five Wimbledon titles, three US Open titles, and three French Open titles among these accomplishments. Djokovic's collection of Grand Slam titles shows how versatile and adaptable he is on different courts, making him a true all-court player.

Djokovic's long time as the best player in the world shows how consistent and tough he is. As of October 2021, he has spent more than 340 weeks at the top of the ATP rankings. This makes him the player with the most weeks at No. 1, overtaking Federer and Nadal. His position as the best player shows how good he is, how tough he is mentally, and how much he cares about the sport.

Djokovic has done well in more than just Grand Slams. He has also done well in ATP Masters 1000 tournaments. Outside of the majors, these prestigious events have the highest level of competition. Djokovic has won 38 Masters 1000 titles, which is more than Nadal, whose previous record was 35. This statistic shows that Djokovic has been excellent all season long.

Djokovic's head-to-head records against his contemporaries and other tennis legends are an important part of his statistical dominance. He has won matches against Federer and Nadal, two other members of the "Big Three." This shows that he can consistently outperform and outsmart his opponents. Djokovic's head-to-head record against many top players shows that he is one of the best athletes to ever play the sport.

At the end of each season, the top eight players compete in what used to be called the ATP Tour Finals but is now called the Nitto ATP Finals. The fact that Djokovic won the tournament shows how good and dominant he is in a very competitive setting. He has won the year-end championships five times, which is the same number Federer has won. Also, in 2015, Djokovic did something that had never been done before: he won every match in the tournament. This showed his perfect form and unmatched dominance.

Novak Djokovic is a genius when it comes to numbers. Djokovic's excellence is clear in many statistical categories, from his Grand Slam wins to his record-breaking time as world No. 1 to his dominance in Masters 1000 tournaments. His great head-to-head records and amazing year-end championships solidify his place as one of the best tennis players of all time. As Djokovic keeps adding to his impressive record, he solidifies his place as one of the best athletes of all time.

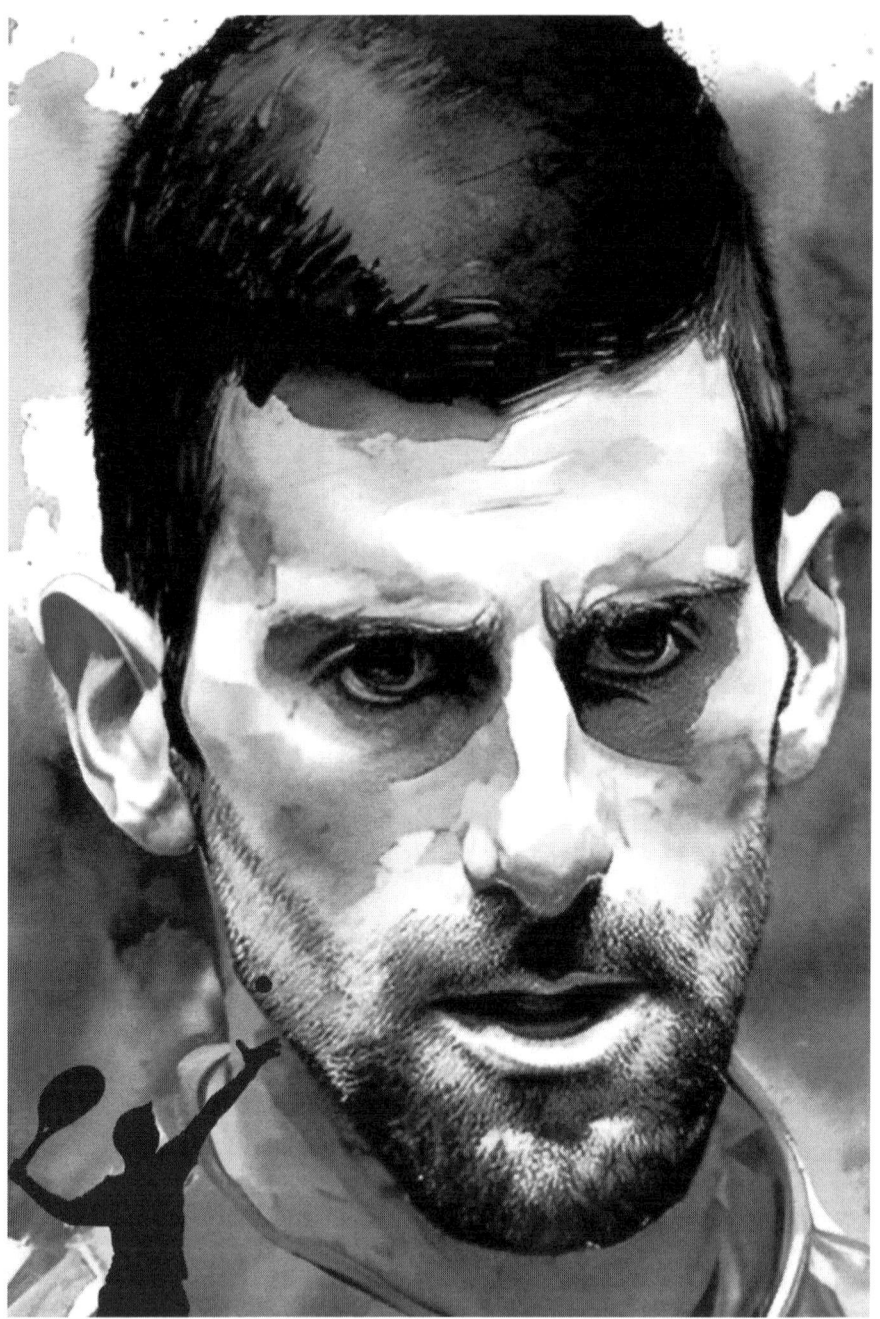

13. The Rise of Novak Djokovic's Business Empire

Novak Djokovic is famous for being a great tennis player, but he is also a smart businessman who has built a thriving empire outside of tennis. This chapter goes into detail about the different business ventures and investments that have made Djokovic so successful. We look at the main things that have helped Djokovic become such a successful businessman, like how much he cares about health and wellness and how well he pays attention to details.

Novak Djokovic's business career started with an idea that went far beyond tennis. Djokovic knew that an athlete's career only lasts so long, so he tried to build a portfolio of businesses that would keep him financially stable after he stopped playing. His main goal was to leave a mark on the world that would last beyond his time as a pro tennis player.

Djokovic went into the health and wellness industry because he was very committed to his own physical and mental health. He started his own line of health supplements, which were carefully made with the help of well-known experts. Djokovic's dedication to quality and the focus of his brand on quality helped him quickly gain a large share of the market.

Djokovic's charisma and status as a powerful person helped him move into the world of fashion and high-end goods. He worked with well-known brands like Lacoste and Seiko to get a lot of high-profile endorsements. By using his fame and marketability to his advantage, Djokovic was able to increase his presence in a number of high-end areas and grow his business empire.

Djokovic also got into real estate because he knew how important it was to have different sources of income. He put his money into prime properties all over the world, choosing places that had the potential for long-term growth and good returns. These projects were not only smart investments, but they also gave Djokovic a chance to grow his business network and relationships.

Djokovic started the Novak Djokovic Foundation because he wanted to do good things outside of business. This branch of his charity works to help poor children in his home country of Serbia get a good education and grow and learn as young children. Through this foundation, Djokovic is able to channel his passion for social change and give future generations the tools they need to make a difference.

Djokovic's business success can be explained in part by his

ability to make strategic alliances. He knows how important it is to surround himself with people and groups that share his core values and goals. These partnerships have opened up new opportunities for Djokovic, allowing him to try new things and reach new markets.

Novak Djokovic's rise to become a business mogul can teach aspiring business owners a lot. His success comes from his unwavering dedication to excellence, his careful attention to details, and his constant desire to make a positive difference. This chapter ends with some of the most important business lessons that can be learned from Djokovic's journey. These include the importance of giving back to society and the need to be persistent.

Novak Djokovic is best known for his achievements in tennis, but his business ventures have been just as impressive. Djokovic has done a great job of building a diverse and successful portfolio of businesses, from health and wellness to fashion and real estate. His journey as a business owner is an example for those who want to reach their full potential on and off the court.

14. Mental Fortitude: The Unbreakable Spirit of Novak Djokovic

Novak Djokovic is a great example of the power of a strong mind and a strong spirit in the world of professional tennis. During his long and successful career, Djokovic has had to deal with a lot of problems, both on and off the court, that have tested his strength and determination. Still, he has won every time, showing that he is not only a great athlete but also a real winner in his mind and spirit.

Novak Djokovic's journey to having a strong mind began when he was young. As a child growing up in war-torn Serbia, he had to deal with problems from an early age. He could have given up on his dreams because of the constant bombings, economic unrest, and lack of resources. But Djokovic's strong will drove him to follow his dream of playing tennis. His mental strength was built on this early determination.

As Djokovic moved into the competitive world of professional tennis, he ran into many problems that could have broken a weaker person. His career was in danger of falling apart because of crushing losses, nagging injuries, and personal problems. But Djokovic saw these problems as chances to learn and get better. Instead of feeling sorry for himself, he used these setbacks as motivation to improve both his physical and mental game. Djokovic's life changed when he realized how important it was to believe in himself. He learned that success on the tennis court was as much about the mind as it was about the body by training hard and working on his mind. Djokovic started to use his inner strength, building a strong belief in his skills and an unshakeable confidence that would become his trademark.

Throughout his career, Djokovic has fought his toughest opponents in epic battles that have pushed the limits of mental strength. Roger Federer and Rafael Nadal are just two of the players he's played against who show how strong he is. Djokovic's ability to handle intense pressure, keep his cool in key moments, and recover from tough situations has helped him turn defeat into victory many times. Even though Djokovic's mental strength shines most on the tennis court, his unwavering spirit isn't limited to the game. His holistic approach to life, which focuses on taking care of the mind, body, and soul, has helped him stay successful. Djokovic's dedication to meditation, a plant-based diet, and a balanced lifestyle show how important it is to take care of yourself and your mind if you want to be successful.

As long as Djokovic keeps being the best tennis player in the world, his strong mind and unbreakable will leave an indelible mark on the sport. His longevity, ability to change, and ability to reach across generations have made him one of the best of all time. Djokovic's unwavering drive and toughness are also an inspiration to aspiring athletes and people from all walks of life. He shows that with the right attitude, anything is possible.In the end, Novak Djokovic's story shows how important it is to have a strong mind and an unbreakable spirit. Djokovic is one of the best tennis players of all time because he never stops believing in himself, can turn setbacks into opportunities, and works hard to improve himself. His story shows that true champions aren't just defined by how good they are physically, but also by how strong their minds are and how determined they are to win.

15. A Comparison between Novak Djokovic and Other Tennis Players

Throughout the history of tennis, there have been many great players. Fans all over the world have been amazed and inspired by these players' incredible skills, hard work, and achievements. Novak Djokovic has shown himself to be a strong player among these others. In this chapter, we'll compare Djokovic to some other famous tennis players, looking at their strengths, weaknesses, playing styles, and accomplishments.

Roger Federer, who is also called "The Maestro" of tennis, is thought to be one of the best players in the history of the sport. Fans have been mesmerized by his elegant and fluid playing style and his beautiful shots for more than 20 years. When we compare Djokovic to Federer, we see that they are different in some ways.

a. Playing style: Federer is known for making shots with ease and grace, while Djokovic is known for his great defensive skills and mental toughness. He usually lasts longer than his opponents because he plays well from the baseline and keeps attacking them.

b. Grand Slam Titles: Federer holds the record for the most Grand Slam titles with 20. Djokovic is close behind with 18 titles. Federer's dominance in the early 2000s set him apart, but Djokovic's recent rise shows that they will be fierce rivals.

Head-to-Head: Djokovic has a slight edge over Federer in their head-to-head matches. Their fights on the court have made for some of the most exciting tennis matches ever.

Rafael Nadal, who is known as "The King of Clay," has

made a name for himself as one of the toughest tennis players. Even Djokovic would have a hard time beating him because of how hard he works and how good he is at defense.

Style of play: Nadal's game is known for his amazing topspin forehand shots and his incredible speed on the court. Djokovic's style is different because he has a strong two-handed backhand and uses strategy to beat opponents.

b. Grand Slam Titles: Nadal has 20 Grand Slam titles, which is the same number as Federer and Djokovic. In this way, Nadal stands out because he is so good on clay courts and has won a record number of French Open titles.

c. Head-to-Head: Djokovic and Nadal have played against each other many times, and their matches are often long and hard. Djokovic's ability to stop Nadal's topspin shots has led to close matches with a lot of action.

Even though Andy Murray has been hurt a lot, he has had a great career and is known for his toughness and fighting spirit on the court. When we look at the differences between Djokovic and Murray, they are interesting.

a. Style of play: Both players have great defensive skills and are willing to outlast their opponents. Murray plays more defensively than Djokovic, but Djokovic's offensive skills and ability to control the game give him the edge.

b. Grand Slam Titles: Djokovic has won the most, with 18, while Murray has won the least, with 3. But Murray's huge efforts to get back on his feet after major physical setbacks and his multiple Olympic medals show how determined he is.

c. Head-to-Head: Djokovic has won most of their matches

against each other. This is because Djokovic plays consistently well and knows how to take advantage of Murray's weaknesses.

When you compare Djokovic to other tennis players, you can see what makes him such a great competitor. Federer, Nadal, and Murray each have their own strengths and accomplishments, but Djokovic stands out because of his mental toughness, defensive skills, and offensive skills. His competition with Federer and Nadal has led to some memorable matches, which has helped him stay at the top of tennis. As long as Djokovic keeps winning trophies, his reputation in the sport will continue to grow.

16. The Key Factors Behind Novak Djokovic's Success and Failure

The road to success is usually full of problems, hard work, and commitment. Novak Djokovic, the tennis star from Serbia, is not new to this idea. During his long and successful career, Djokovic has had many wins and losses, each of which was shaped by important factors that led to his success or failure. In this chapter, we'll take a closer look at these factors to find out what helped Djokovic reach the top of his sport and what held him back.

A. Key Factor in Success - Mental Resilience

Novak Djokovic's mental toughness is one of the things that has made his career stand out. The key to Djokovic's success has been his ability to stay calm, focused, and determined under pressure. Djokovic has always shown a strong mind, whether it was getting over injuries, coming back from losing positions in matches, or staying motivated when things were hard.

Djokovic's ability to keep his mind strong was shown in the 2011 Australian Open final against Andy Murray. Djokovic was down two sets to none, but he didn't give up hope. With a strong will, he came back to win the next three sets and the championship in the end. This incredible show of mental toughness has become a trademark of Djokovic's career and makes him a very tough opponent on the tennis court.

B. <u>Key Factor in Failure - Lack of Consistency</u>

Djokovic's mental toughness has been a huge part of his success, but his lack of consistency has sometimes hurt him. In his quest to be the best, Djokovic has had many times when he couldn't keep up a consistent level of play. These changes in form have caused him to lose and miss out on opportunities, which has kept him from reaching his full potential.

In 2017, when he didn't defend his Wimbledon title, Djokovic's lack of consistency stood out. Djokovic had a great start to the year, winning the Australian Open and making it to the final of the French Open. But then everything stopped. He lost in the Wimbledon quarterfinals because he made a lot of mistakes that were out of character for him. This unexpected loss was a stark reminder of how vulnerable Djokovic can be when his game changes.

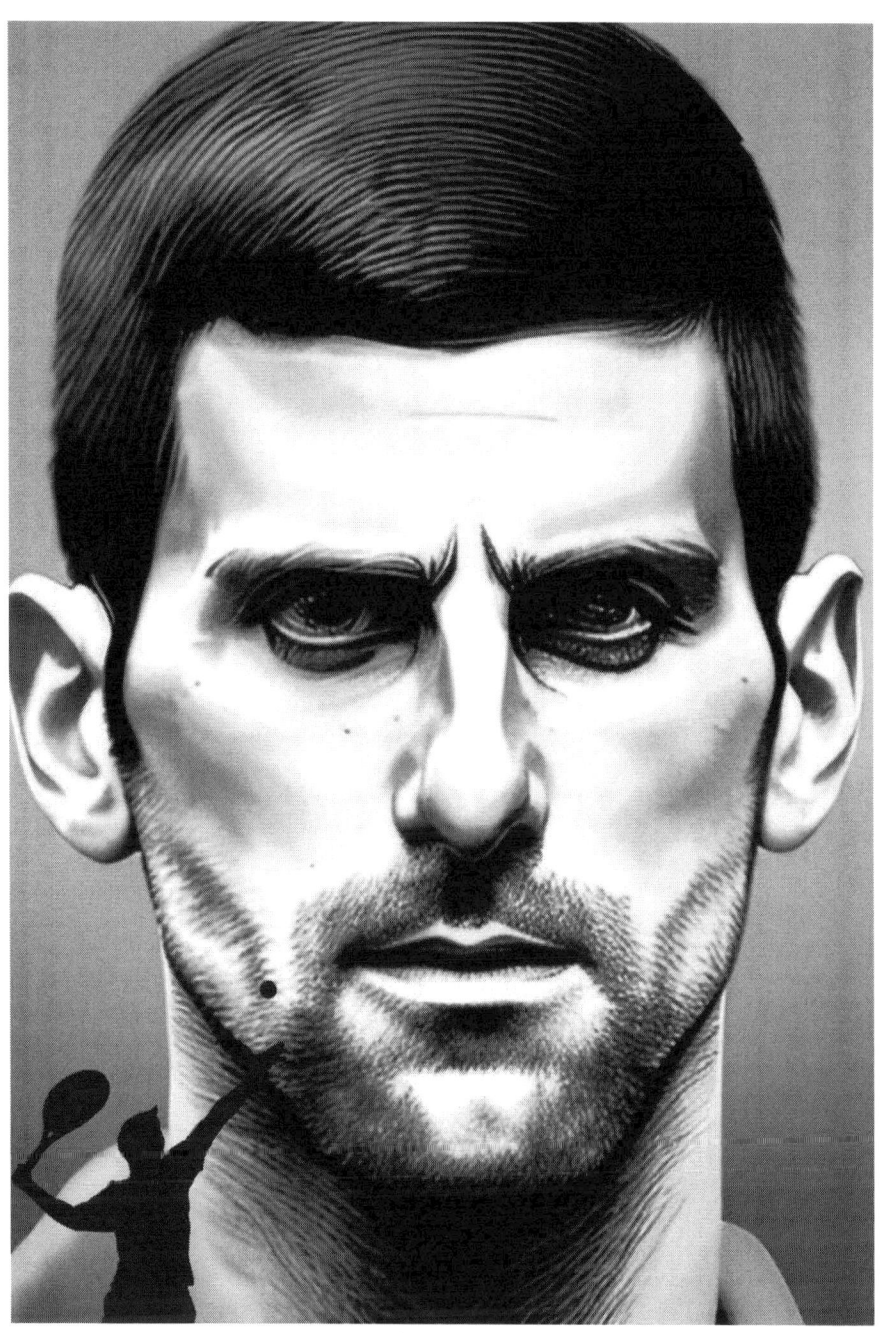

C. **Balancing Success and Failure**

Novak Djokovic's career shows how difficult it is to separate success and failure in an athlete's life. He has been able to get back on his feet after setbacks because he has a strong mind. He is also very determined to overcome any problems that come his way. But his lack of consistency has also slowed him down and kept him from reaching many of the highest points of his potential.

Even though Djokovic's career has had both successes and failures, he has always shown a strong commitment to bettering himself. By recognizing and learning from the things that lead to success and failure, Djokovic keeps getting better and keeps pushing the limits of what he can do.

Djokovic's journey can teach aspiring athletes and anyone else who wants to be great a lot, whether it's about how strong his mind is or how hard it is for him to stay consistent. His story shows how important it is to adapt, learn, and keep going through the ups and downs of life. In the end, this leads to personal growth and the chance to do great things.

17. The Art of Style Play: Decoding Novak Djokovic's Signature Tennis Fashion

Novak Djokovic is a famous tennis player from Serbia. He is known not only for his great skills and amazing athleticism on the court, but also for his unique and fascinating style of play. In this chapter, we'll get into Djokovic's fashion choices and look at how his sense of style adds to and improves his performance. We will look at the key parts of Djokovic's signature style and see how they affect his game.

Novak Djokovic's style is known for being lively and colorful. He often wears bright, striking colors like electric blue, bright yellow, and striking green, which match his personality and make him look confident. This choice of bright colors helps Djokovic stand out on the court and make sure that everyone is looking at him. This has a big psychological effect, as his opponents may be momentarily distracted or feel like they can't handle his strength.

Djokovic gives equal importance to both style and functionality. He likes fabrics that improve performance by letting air in, being flexible, and getting rid of sweat. With long hours of hard physical work and tough match conditions, Djokovic has to be able to adapt to changing weather and stay comfortable throughout the game. Modern fabrics are used to make his clothes more flexible, so he can move around more easily and keep his mind on his game.

Every part of Djokovic's clothes is carefully made to fit him just right. From the way his shirts are cut to the way his shorts are made, Djokovic's clothes create a silhouette that shows off how athletic he is. Because his clothes are so well-fitted, he can move freely and easily on the court without any restrictions. This attention to detail extends to his tennis shoes, which are made to give him the best support, stability, and grip. This gives him an advantage when he needs to change directions quickly or move quickly and quickly.

Novak Djokovic knows that the right accessories can make or break a tennis outfit. He often wears a distinctive visor that protects his eyes from the sun's glare and lets him see well during games. The visor is both useful and stylish because it adds another piece to his well-put-together look. The strap of his visor often matches the color of his outfit, which shows how much Djokovic cares about the little things.

Novak Djokovic is not only a genius on the tennis court, but he is also a fashion artist. His style choices are thoughtful, new, and on purpose. By wearing clothes with bright colors, functional fabrics, and perfect tailoring, Djokovic makes an impression that goes well with his performance on the court. Because he pays attention to the little things, every part of his outfit has a purpose and makes him look better as a whole. As Djokovic keeps making a name for himself in tennis, his style play continues to be a big part of his success, inspiring both tennis fans and fashionistas.

18. The Unstoppable Legacy of Novak Djokovic

Novak Djokovic, a tennis prodigy from Serbia, wowed the world with his amazing skills, unwavering determination, and incredible consistency. As we learn more about this amazing athlete's history, we look at how Djokovic's undeniable talent, hard work ethic, and unbreakable spirit have helped him make a name for himself in tennis history.

Novak Djokovic's journey in tennis began when he was young. His parents helped him get started because they saw his talent and encouraged his interest. From the start, Djokovic showed a level of intensity on the court that was unmatched. He challenged his opponents and pushed himself to the limit to do well. In 2008, he won his first Grand Slam at the Australian Open. This was the moment that put him on the international stage.

One thing that makes Djokovic stand out is that he can change his game to fit any opponent or situation. His speed, adaptability, and strategic thinking make him a tough opponent who can find weaknesses in even the most difficult situations. Djokovic has changed his game so that he can win on any surface, whether it's through his great serve returns, subtle drop shots, or impenetrable defense.

During his career, Djokovic has had great rivalries with great tennis players like Rafael Nadal and Roger Federer. The battles between these three legends on the court have wowed fans and shown how much talent there is in the sport. These players' fierce competition and mutual respect have pushed Djokovic to strive for greatness, which has raised the level of tennis as a whole.

Djokovic has always been very proud of his Serbian heritage. As a famous athlete, he has become a source of inspiration for his countrymen. He has encouraged a whole generation of young athletes to dream big and work hard to reach their goals. The constant support he gets from his fellow Serbs makes him even more determined to do amazing things.

As of 2021, Djokovic has won 20 Grand Slam titles. This makes him one of the best tennis players of all time. Because he never stopped trying to be the best, he has won trophies at all four majors, including nine Australian Opens, five Wimbledons, and three US Opens. Djokovic's strong desire to be considered one of the best players of all time drives him to keep breaking records.

Djokovic's success isn't just because of his amazing physical skills; it's also because of how strong he is mentally.

Throughout his career, Djokovic has faced problems, injuries, and setbacks, but he has never given up. This has helped him overcome mental obstacles and come back stronger. This mental toughness, along with his unwavering self-belief, has helped him win many times despite problems that seemed impossible to solve.

In addition to what he's done on the court, Djokovic's charitable work says a lot about who he is. Through the Novak Djokovic Foundation, he wants to help poor children in Serbia and around the world get a better education and better health care. Even though he has won many awards, Djokovic stays humble and always thanks his team, fans, and opponents. He is a great example of true sportsmanship.

Novak Djokovic's legacy is one of unmatched skill, incredible toughness, and unwavering drive. He is one of the best tennis players of all time because of what he did on the court, how many records he set, and how hard he worked at his craft. As Djokovic continues to defy expectations and push the limits of his sport, his inspiring journey will show the power of hard work, dedication, and the never-ending pursuit of excellence.

19. The Private Life of Novak Djokovic

As the sun goes down over the beautiful city of Belgrade, Novak Djokovic can finally leave the pressures of the tennis court behind and go back to his private life. Away from the cameras and the fans who love him, Novak enjoys the simple things that give him peace of mind and keep him working hard to be the best.

Novak's private life revolves around his family. His love and devotion to his wife, Jelena, and their two children, Stefan and Tara, are a constant source of motivation. When Novak gets off the tennis court, his main job is to be a loving husband and father. This is what he was always meant to be.

Novak and Jelena have been together since they were

teenagers, so they have a strong bond that can't be broken. They encourage and help each other on their own paths, whether Novak is trying to get better at tennis or Jelena is trying to help others. Together, they create a balance that makes their souls feel good.

Novak finds comfort in simple things like cooking for his family in the privacy of their home. He thinks that cooking is a way to not only feed the body but also connect with his roots and bring people together. Novak often plays the role of a culinary artist, putting love and creativity into every meal he makes, whether he's making traditional Serbian dishes or trying out new dishes from around the world.

Novak cares about his spiritual and emotional health as he tries to improve himself. Meditation, yoga, and being mindful are all important parts of his daily schedule.

These habits give him a sense of stability and help him find clarity in the chaos of his busy schedule. Novak is seen by the world as a fierce competitor, but his private life shows that he is a calm, thoughtful person.

Novak is very committed to helping people outside of his family and personal life. The Novak Djokovic Foundation was started in 2007 to help poor children in Serbia get a better education and more opportunities. Every time Novak isn't playing tennis, he has a chance to help other people and give them hope, just like tennis gave him hope.

But it's not easy to keep a private life when people are always looking at you. Paparazzi follow Novak everywhere he goes, hoping to get a look at his private life. But he still does his best to keep his family's privacy and find a good balance between his public and private selves.

Novak Djokovic's private life shows that he has many sides to his personality. Behind the fierce competitor and sports icon is a loving husband, a caring father, a spiritual seeker, and a generous person with a big heart. In this chapter, we got a glimpse of a man who does well not only on the tennis court but also in quiet moments with his family, where his true greatness shows.

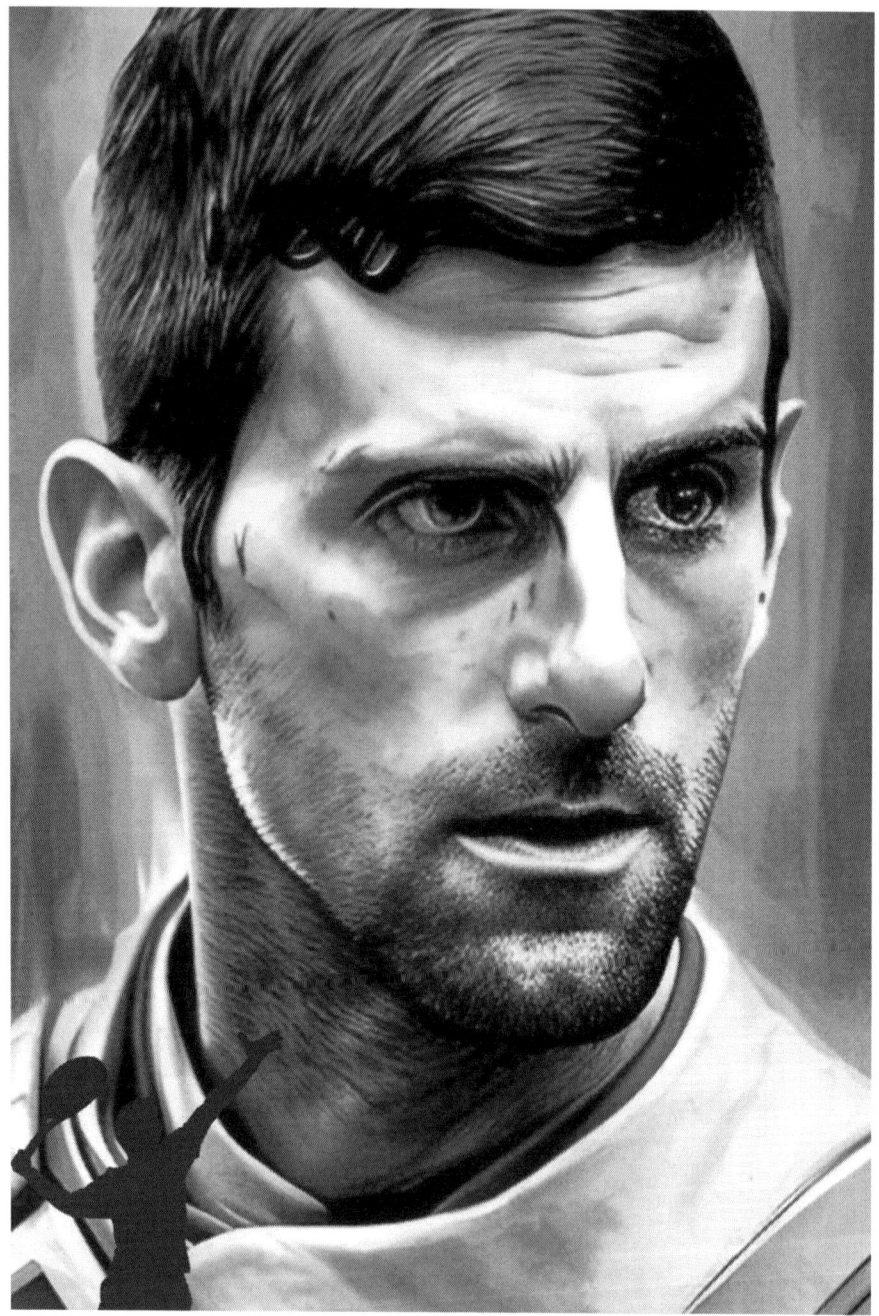

20. The Unfathomable Fortune of Novak Djokovic

Novak Djokovic is one of the most famous tennis players in the world. Djokovic is one of the best tennis players of all time because he has skills that are unmatched, is determined, and stays focused. But his incredible wealth, both on and off the court, is the reason he has been so successful and driven to be the best.

Djokovic was born in Belgrade, Serbia, on May 22, 1987. He grew up in a country torn by war and with few resources. Like many people who want to be athletes, he had to deal with a lot of problems and hard times when he was young. Even with all of these problems, Djokovic never gave up on his dreams and worked hard to follow his passion for tennis.

He had no idea that his constant hard work would lead to huge success and astronomical wealth. As soon as Djokovic turned pro, he quickly became the best tennis player in the world, winning Grand Slam titles and setting records along the way. He got to the top of his sport because he was a great athlete, a fierce competitor, and a smart strategist.

With each victory, Djokovic's wealth grew at a very fast rate. Prize money from tournaments poured in, sponsorship offers poured in, and lucrative endorsement deals followed. As one of the most marketable athletes in the world, Djokovic became the face of many well-known brands, from luxury watches to sports equipment, which helped him make a lot of money.

But his success wasn't the only thing that made him rich. Djokovic's mental strength and ability to keep going through hard times helped him on and off the court. He turned his mistakes into important lessons that helped him come back stronger than ever. Djokovic's amazing good luck, both financially and spiritually, grew because he was able to turn failures into wins.

But Djokovic is not the type to keep his money to himself. Djokovic is known for his charitable work, and he uses his money to help other people in positive ways. Through his foundation, he works to improve early childhood education, give all children the same chances, and help communities that have been hit by natural disasters. His determination to make a difference shows how deep he is as a person and how lucky he is.

As the rest of the tennis world watches in awe, Djokovic never stops trying to be the best and getting what he wants. Even though he has a lot of money, he still wants more. He keeps pushing the limits of what is possible on the tennis court.

Djokovic's story is an example for all of us. It shows that anyone can achieve success and wealth if they are determined, passionate, and stay focused.

In the end, Novak Djokovic's wealth is really hard to understand. From his humble beginnings in war-torn Serbia to his status as a tennis legend and global icon, his life is a great example of how hard work and ambition can pay off. Djokovic's wealth isn't just based on how much money he has. It's also based on how he affects the world and how much he inspires so many people. Novak Djokovic's incredible luck will undoubtedly continue to shape his legacy for many years to come.

21. The Unparalleled Records of Novak Djokovic

Novak Djokovic's name is synonymous with great tennis players and records that have never been broken. He has captivated the world with his amazing skills, unmatched consistency, and unwavering drive. Djokovic is thought to be one of the best tennis players of all time, and his career is full of records that cement his place in the history of the sport. In this chapter, we go into detail about the Serbian maestro's amazing records, which show off his amazing skills and unwavering dedication.

Grand Slam Glory: Djokovic's dominance at Grand Slam tournaments has been nothing short of amazing. As of 2021, he has won 20 Grand Slam singles titles, which is the same number as his biggest rivals Roger Federer and Rafael Nadal. Djokovic was the first male player in the Open

Era to win the Career Grand Slam on three different surfaces (hardcourt, clay, and grass). Also, he was the first player in the Open Era to win four Grand Slam tournaments in a row in two different seasons. This is called the "Nole Slam."

2. Soar on Hardcourts: Djokovic's record-breaking performances show that he likes playing on hardcourts. He holds the record for the most hardcourt titles in the Open Era, with an amazing number of ATP Masters 1000 titles. Also, in 2015, Djokovic won all nine ATP Masters 1000 tournaments, making him the first and only player in history to reach this historic milestone.

Masters of the Masters: Djokovic has left an indelible mark on the ATP Masters 1000 tournaments, outperforming his peers with a record that can't be beat. As of 2021, Djokovic has won the most titles, 36. This is more than Rafael Nadal, who held the record before Djokovic. His success in these top-level tournaments shows how consistent he is and how well he can play at the highest level on different surfaces.

4. The Year-End No. 1 Streaks: Djokovic's consistency was shown by the fact that he ended each year as the best player in the world. From 2011 to 2015 and again from 2018 to 2020, he was the best player in the ATP rankings at the end of each year. This was an amazing six-year run. This show of skill showed not only how good he was, but also how he could keep doing his best for a long time.

5. Winning Against the Best: Djokovic's ability to beat the best players in the world shows how tough he is mentally. He has a winning record against two of the best tennis players of all time, Roger Federer and Rafael Nadal. Djokovic's ability to always step up to the challenge and

do better than his opponents makes him one of the most impressive players the sport has ever seen.

6. Weeks at No.1: In March 2021, Djokovic broke Roger Federer's record for most weeks as the world's best player. He has held this record for more than 320 weeks and keeps adding to it, making him the best example of excellence and dominance over time.

Novak Djokovic's name will always be written in the tennis record books. His unmatched consistency, never-ending desire to win, and technical skill have helped him have an amazing career with a lot of records. With every new record he breaks, Djokovic cements his place as one of the best athletes of all time. As we keep seeing him do great things, we can't help but wonder what other records he will break and how his legacy will continue to grow.

22. The Enigmatic Persona of Novak Djokovic

Novak Djokovic has made a name for himself as one of the best and most interesting athletes of all time in the world of professional tennis. Djokovic's rise to the top of the tennis world has been nothing short of amazing. He has a unique mix of athleticism, skill, and mental toughness that no one else has. Fans are drawn to him not only because of how good he is on the court, but also because of how mysterious he is and how interesting his profile is. In this chapter, we go deeper into Novak Djokovic's personality and look at the different things that make him such a great athlete.

To get a sense of who Novak Djokovic is, you have to look at his early life and upbringing. Djokovic was born on May 22, 1987, in Belgrade, Serbia. Even when he was young, he liked tennis. He grew up in a loving family, and his parents saw his talent early on and encouraged his love of the sport. Growing up in war-torn Serbia didn't make Djokovic's path to success easy, but it had a big impact on who he became as a person.

One thing that makes Djokovic who he is is that he is always competitive and determined. Djokovic is known for his hard work ethic and never-give-up attitude. His tenacity on the court is often credited as a key reason for his many comebacks and grand slam wins. He does well under pressure and always pushes himself to the limit, which makes him a strong player on any court.

Djokovic is also different from other tennis players because he has a strong mind. This mental strength lets him deal with setbacks and keep his mind on the task at hand, even when things are hard. Djokovic's ability to ignore distractions and stay calm under pressure has helped him last longer than his opponents and win important matches.

Even though Djokovic is known for having a strong mind, his emotions on the court often show a different side of his personality. Djokovic always shows how he feels, whether it's through his joyous celebrations or his angry outbursts. These emotional outbursts endear him to his fans and give him an extra layer of mystery. They show how passionate and intense he is.

Djokovic is known for his competitive spirit and emotional outbursts, but he is also very humble and has a strong desire to give back to society. He is known for his generosity and charitable work, and he uses his platform to do good things outside of the court. Djokovic's desire to make a difference gives him more depth as a person and shows a caring side that fans and critics alike can relate to.

Djokovic's interesting personality comes from his many interests outside of tennis. He reads a lot, promotes living a healthy life, and does both meditation and yoga. These parts of Djokovic's life show more about his deep-seated desire to learn and grow as a person.

Novak Djokovic's profile and personality show a unique mix of competitiveness, mental toughness, on-court emotions, humility, and many different interests. These traits are a big part of why he is so good at tennis and why he has made an impact both on and off the court. Understanding Djokovic's complicated personality helps us appreciate his achievements more and gives us a glimpse of the unbreakable spirit that pushes him to reach new heights in the world of professional tennis.

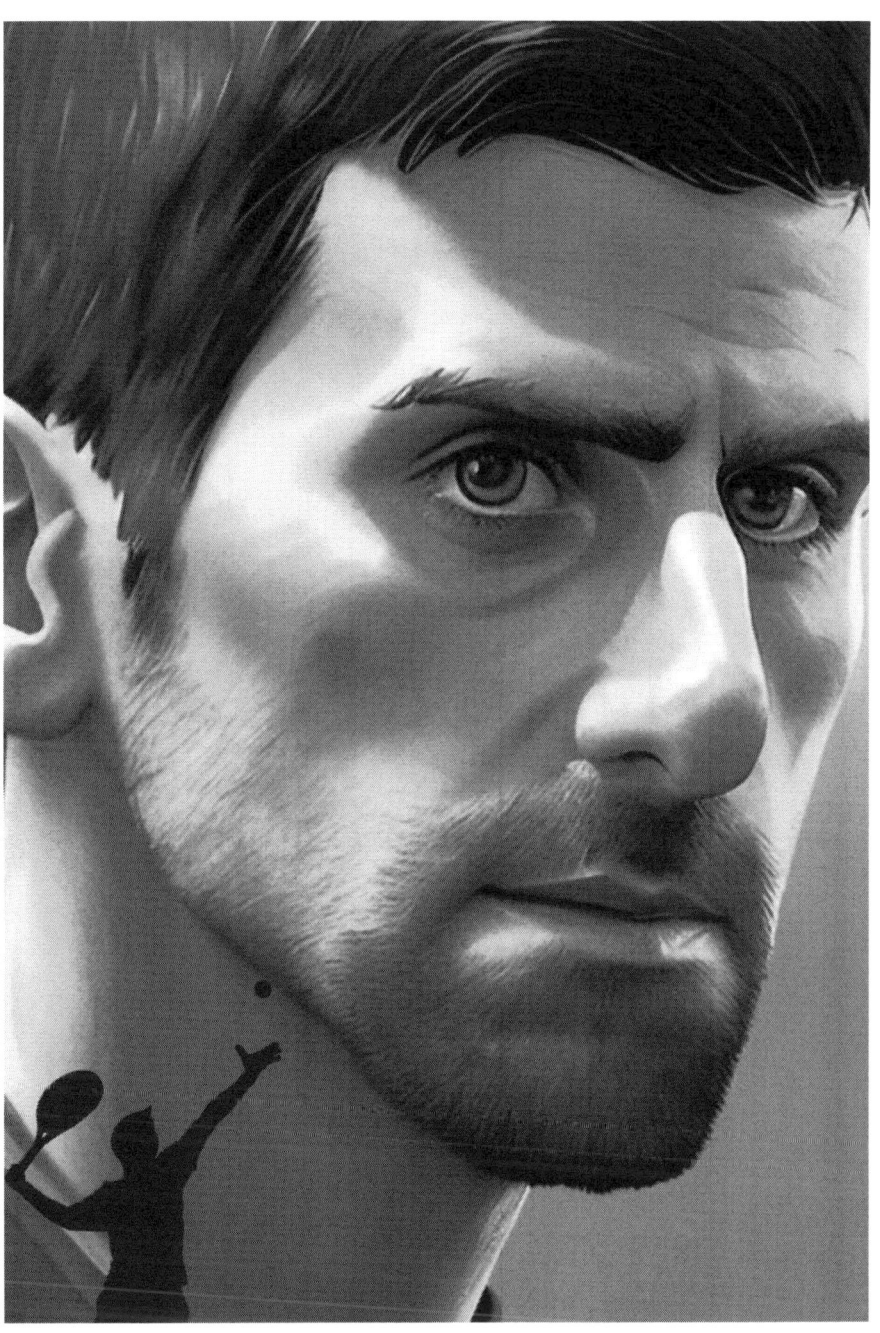

23. The Journey to Becoming Like Novak Djokovic

In this chapter, we'll look at how Novak Djokovic, one of the best tennis players in the world, went from being a kid to becoming one of the best. Djokovic's drive, discipline, and passion have helped him become a great tennis player, and we'll look more closely at what makes him so successful. If you think like him and do what he did, you can put yourself on the right track to reach your full potential in tennis or anything else you choose.

Novak Djokovic has always said that setting goals is important. The first step to getting what you want is to know what it is you want. As a kid, you should start by making goals that are specific, measurable, attainable, relevant, and have a deadline. Break your long-term goal of becoming as good as Djokovic into shorter-term goals that you can reach. This will let you see how far you've come and keep you going along the way.

One thing that makes Djokovic stand out is that he is very disciplined. To be like him, you have to make a promise to put your training first and always do your best. Having a set schedule on and off the court will help you develop the discipline you need to be successful. Set up a daily routine that includes working out, practicing your tennis skills, learning about the game, and taking care of your overall health.

Djokovic practices harder than anyone else. He spends a lot of time practicing and always wants to get better. Make every minute count when you're on the court. Be there and pay attention during drills, games, and training. Work on your weaknesses and get better at what you're good at. Accept challenges and don't settle for average. Remember that the level of your performance is based on how well you practice.

Success in tennis, like success in life, requires a strong mind. Djokovic's ability to deal with stress and get back on his feet after a loss is a valuable lesson. Develop a growth mindset, which means you know that failure is not the end, but a chance to get better. Build your mental strength by doing things like visualizing, being mindful, and talking to yourself in a positive way. Remember that it's not always about winning. What matters is how you deal with losing and what you learn from it.

To be like Djokovic, you need to be physically fit. His amazing stamina, agility, and strength allow him to win even the most difficult fights. Do a well-rounded fitness routine that includes exercises for your heart, your muscles, and your flexibility. Eat a well-balanced diet to give your body the fuel it needs, and always put recovery and rest first to avoid getting hurt.

Novak Djokovic gets ideas from many different places, and you should, too. Surround yourself with people who share your goals and will help you on your journey. Read biographies and watch documentaries about great athletes who have been through hard times and come out on top. You can go to professional tennis matches in person or watch them on TV or live. Use every chance to get a spark of motivation and drive yourself toward your goals.

To be like Novak Djokovic, you have to work hard, be disciplined, and keep trying to get better. You can reach your full potential like Djokovic did by setting goals, being disciplined, practicing with a purpose, getting mentally tough, putting physical fitness first, and looking for inspiration.

Remember that the journey may be hard, but it will be worth it in the end. So, put on your tennis shoes, have faith in yourself, and start this amazing journey to become as good as Novak Djokovic.

24. The Multi-Faceted World of Novak Djokovic's Hobbies

Novak Djokovic, a tennis star from Serbia, is known all over the world for his amazing skills on the court. But Djokovic isn't just good at tennis. He also spends a lot of time on a variety of hobbies that bring him joy, relaxation, and personal fulfillment. In this chapter, we look at Novak Djokovic's many interests and get a glimpse of how he spends his time when he's not on the tennis court.

Djokovic's devotion to meditation and other mind-body practices is one of the things that people know him for. He thinks that these ways of calming down are a big part of why he is so good at tennis. They help him focus, reduce stress, and keep his mind clear. Djokovic talks a lot about how important it is to be in the moment, and he meditates every day to make sure his mind is as healthy as his body.

Djokovic is a strong believer in the power of a healthy, well-balanced diet. Together with his wife, Jelena, he started a plant-based restaurant called "Eqvita" in Monaco. The restaurant focuses on the importance of choosing sustainable, organic, and nourishing foods. Djokovic eats a gluten-free and dairy-free diet, which he thinks is a big part of why he is so healthy and has such great endurance on the court.

Djokovic spends a lot of his free time reading, as he is always looking to learn and grow as a person. He likes to read books that teach him about spirituality, psychology, and how to improve himself. Djokovic has talked about how books like "The Power of Now" by Eckhart Tolle and "Autobiography of a Yogi" by Paramahansa Yogananda have changed his view of the world and made him stronger mentally.

Djokovic has a strong commitment to helping people outside of his own interests. The main goal of his Novak Djokovic Foundation is to help poor children in Serbia get a good education and grow and learn when they are young. Djokovic is sure that education can change lives and is committed to making sure that every child, no matter where they come from or how much money they have, has a chance at a better future.

Outside of tennis, Djokovic's biggest joy is being a good father and husband. He cares most about spending quality time with his wife and children. Djokovic loves spending time with his family, whether they are playing sports, going swimming, or just hanging out at home. He finds comfort in their company.

As an athlete who competes around the world, Djokovic has had the chance to learn about different cultures, traditions, and landscapes. He often jumps at the chance to learn about the culture of a place and see its natural beauty. Traveling lets him see things from different points of view, broaden his horizons, and understand how his work affects people all over the world.

Novak Djokovic's hobbies show how he looks at life as a whole. For example, he practices mindfulness and helps others. Whether he's looking for inner peace or trying to make a positive difference in the world, Djokovic's many interests give him depth and make him a more interesting person. They also help him on and off the tennis court.

Conclusion

In conclusion, Novak Djokovic's biography gives a detailed look at his life and career as one of the best tennis players of all time. We learned a lot about Djokovic's early life, his rise to the top of the tennis world, and the struggles he had to overcome to get where he is now from the book's detailed account. From his humble beginnings in war-torn Serbia to his relentless pursuit of excellence on the tennis court, Djokovic's story is one of persistence, passion, and unwavering dedication.

The book shows that Djokovic is very determined and has a lot of mental strength, which helps him overcome both physical and personal problems. It goes into his unique way of thinking and shows how his mindfulness practices, such as meditation and visualization, have been key to his success. The biography also praises Djokovic's unwavering commitment to a plant-based diet. This shows his holistic approach to health and how it has helped his physical and mental health. It's a good reminder of how important a healthy way of life is for peak performance and overall happiness.

The biography also looks at Djokovic's rivalry with tennis legends Roger Federer and Rafael Nadal. It's an interesting look at how these three great athletes interact with each other and how they've affected each other's careers.Overall, Novak Djokovic's life story is an inspiration for people who want to be athletes or have big dreams.

It teaches us the value of hard work, persistence, and self-belief. It also reminds us that success isn't just measured by how many wins we get, but by how strong we are and how we act when things don't go our way. Novak Djokovic's story is a great example of how the power of the human spirit can help people achieve great things.

Printed in Great Britain
by Amazon